MODEL OF A CITY IN CIVIL WAR

MODEL OF A CITY IN CIVIL WAR

poems by adam day

Sarabande  Books
LOUISVILLE, KENTUCKY

THE LINDA BRUCKHEIMER SERIES IN KENTUCKY LITERATURE

Please direct inquiries to:

Managing Editor
Sarabande Books, Inc.
2234 Dundee Road, Suite 200
Louisville, KY 40205

Library of Congress Cataloging-in-Publication Data

Day, Adam, 1977–
[Poems. Selections]
Model of a city in civil war : poems / Adam Day.—First edition.
pages cm
ISBN 978-1-941411-02-5 (pbk. : alk. paper)
I. Title.
PS3604.A9798A6 2015
811'.6—dc23
                              2014028848

Cover by Jonathan Graf.

Interior by Kirkby Gann Tittle.

Manufactured in Canada.

This book is printed on acid-free paper.

Sarabande Books is a nonprofit literary organization.

The Kentucky Arts Council, the state arts agency, supports Sarabande Books with state tax dollars and federal funding from the National Endowment for the Arts.

CON

ACKNOWLEDGEMENTS

Grateful acknowledgement to the editors of the following publications, where these poems, sometimes in different versions, first appeared:

AGNI: "The Children, the Grass" (published as [Here are the Children]") and "Combine"

Antioch Review: "Hiding Again, in London"

Carolina Quarterly: "His Dementia"

Columbia: A Journal of Literature & Art: "Sarclet" and "Dakota"

Colorado Review: "Condensation Cube"

Copper Nickel: "Blind Attis"

Crab Orchard Review: "Snow in a Gdansk Courtyard"

dcomP magazine: "The Revolution"

FIELD: "Water from the Same Source"

Forklift: Ohio: "He Speaks of Old Age" (published as "Old Age")

Gulf Coast: "Anoosh's Obituary for Himself, to His Son"

Handsome: "The Mayor in Sky Blue Socks" (published as "[Deer herd in the icy fields]")

Hotel Amerika: "Apprehended at a Distance" (published as "[The colorless lake, buoy bells in fog]") and "Model of a City in Civil War" (published as "[A diorama of a city in civil war]")

Indiana Review: "Fårö" (published as "The Dinner Party")

iO: A Journal of New American Poetry: "Time Away" (published as "Shark and Dog")

Jelly Fish: "Elebade"

Kenyon Review: "Diorama—(Scarlet and Liver)" (published as "Gallows Portraits") and "Family Romance"

Madison Review: "Sleeping with Uncle Lester"

Mid-American Review: "The Kinghorse Butchertown Brawl"

Louisville Review: "Strapping"

Margie and *Verse Daily*: "The Cow"

Meridian: "Before the War"

New Madrid and *Verse Daily*: "Clean Lines, Diffuse Lighting" (as "Mother's Hair")

New Orleans Review: "The Insomniac"

North American Review: "We Lived Above a Key Shop"

Pebble Lake: "The Leaving" and "Winter Inventory"

Poetry London: "A Plateau of Excellence"

Roanoke Review: "Coming In at Night" (as "Coming In from the Back Porch at
          Night")

Salt Hill: "Orr's Island"

Still: "Washing My Old Man" (as "Washing Father's Feet") and "Now and Forever"
     (as "Badger Philosphes")

Subtropics: "In Mourning" (as "Badger in Mourning")

Sycamore Review: "A Polite History" and " " (as "[From such material it is almost
          impossible . . .]")

Third Coast: "Smoke"

Third Coast: "Winter Fever" (published as "The Good Winter")

TYPO: "Unease"

The following poems first appeared in the chapbook, *Badger, Apocrypha*, published
as part of the Poetry Society of America's Chapbook Fellowship series: "Winter
Nights," "The Revolution," and "In Mourning."

My deep thanks to the wonderful team at Sarabande, and to everyone else who has
supported me and my writing, many of whom I have the honor to call friend: Philip
Levine, David Alworth, Ellyn Lichvar, my son Alistair Day, Kathleen Graber, Cathy
Wagner, Cal Bedient, Fritz Ward, G.C. Waldrep, Bruce Smith, Hannah Gamble,
Ashley Capps, Rebecca Morgan Frank, Tom Sleigh, Sarah Arvio, David Lehman,
James Tate, Heather Patterson, Aleks Karlsons, Kathleen Driskell, David Baker,
Sumita Chakraborty, Sven Birkerts, Timothy Donnelly, Jeffrey Skinner, Breth Fletcher
Lauer, David Lynn, Alice Quinn, Maurice Manning, Jillian Weise, Don Bogen, Joshua
Poteat, Tony Hoagland, Sally Connelly, Martha Greenwald, Josh English, Jeff Hipsher,
Ben Lord, Philip White, Lisa Williams, Jason Schniederman, Michael Estes, David
Harrity, Kyle Coma Thompson, Broc Rossell, Mark Neely, Greg and Beth Steinbock,

Gayann and Robert Day, Elizabeth Hamsley, Tony Hamsley, Sam Sims, Ken Walker, Michael Cooley, Scott Ward, Jay Baron Nicorvo, Mitchell Waters, Taylor Roberts, John James, Jessica Farquhar, Amy Attaway, Jessica Worthem, Anthony Carelli, Colleen Ammerman, Will Lobko, Madeline Schwartz, Robin LaMer Rahija, Makalani Bandele, Sean Patrick Hill, Duncan Barlow, Kathy Barbour, Kari Kalve, Alen Hamza, David Ebenbach, Kyle McCord, Ellie Schilling, and the crew at Carmichael's Bookstore in Louisville.

Special thanks to the Poetry Society of America, New York University, the University of Houston, and to the Kentucky Arts Council for their generous support.

Thus is order ensured: some have to play the game because they cannot otherwise live, and those who could live otherwise are kept out because they do not want to play the game.

—Theodor Adorno

The house itself is none of these appearances: it is . . . the geometrized projection of these perspectives and of all possible perspectives, that is, the perspectiveless position from which all can be derived . . . not the house seen from nowhere, but the house seen from everywhere.

—Maurice Merleau-Ponty

Model of a City in Civil War

BEFORE THE WAR

I was a woman before the war—
we took the arms of our enemies

and swung them from our crotches.
And lived with them there

until, like ticks, they grew inward, and we
were the first men. But we didn't want

those stolen limbs anymore, and so tried
by force to give them back, hoping

the fists would come alive inside
women and grab hold. But when we were done

the arms only hung dumbly
between our tired legs, shrinking in time—

a useless door handle, a hung shadow
we walk upon.

MODEL OF A CITY IN CIVIL WAR

Men carry a mattress retrieved
        from a dumpster past the flooded

foundations of an unfinished
        high-rise, an old woman catches

a pigeon in the folds of her dress,
        the dead smile and rise from swimming

pools or stand at attention
        on stamps. The landscape can't believe

it's real—there is no ground
        beneath it, like what mirrors do.

The velvet-curtained walls
        of a movie theater. On screen

the hanged men speak
        to one another from broken

necks, and the aspen leaves
        show white in the dark.

COMBINE

Captain Nazret helped the Communists overthrow Haile
         Selassie and when
he discovered his wife's infidelities sewed her into bed
         as she slept

and moved his family to the Isle of Man, where he retired
         and began losing
his mind, so that one All Hallows' he pasted a mustache
         onto the pastor's

sorrel mare and rode it through the cobbled streets of Cregneash
         saying to the costumed kids,
"Come pet comrade Stalin." Children loved the old
         syphilitic because

he'd show them his stomach's gnarled track of surgery scars, because
         of the violet-backed
sunbird he kept until the neighbor's cat, with wet green eyes,
         reached a paw

through the cage bars, and snagged the bird on one hooked claw
         so that a crosshatch
of feathers and blood tattooed the tile floor. That night kids drugged
         the Siamese

with cough medicine and stapled it by the scruff to its owner's
         picket fence.

·

On a Siberian expedition, Nikolai Bryukhanov brought the wrong
      food for the sledge-dogs,
so they had to be killed. But not by the squeamish Commissar.
      On the third day

of Bryukhanov's trial, Stalin sent a note with accompanying
      illustration that read:
"To the members of the Politburo, For all the sins, past and present, hang B.
      by the balls. If they

hold out, consider him acquitted by trial. If they don't, drown him
      in the river."

·

Here sits Queen Anne at Hockley Hole, London
      for the dog and bull show.
A rope is tied 'round the root of the bull's horns and fastened
      to an iron stake,

its slobbery gray nose blown full of pepper to enrage it before
      it's baited. Meanwhile,
men hold dogs by the ears. Let loose, the goal for the dog is to hold for all
      hell to the bull's

snout—the most sensitive spot other than the genitals—"If a bull had balls
      hanging from its face

they'd be attached to his snout." Now, either the dog remains
        fixed, or is thrown

tearing out the flesh it has laid teeth on. The bull, a skeptic in dialogue
        with hope, works
to slide a horn under the cur's belly, and throw it, so that a dog's side
        is often ripped open

entrails protruding like wet sausage—"Yes, it provides much joy
        for the community,
and the animals certainly gain a sense of dignity in achievement."

•

Goya's "Portrait of the Family of Charles IV": intermarriage preserved
        the family's wealth
and the compact features of mongoloids. Deformed by a hunting accident,
        Charles—subsidiary

to his wife, his mouth full of gravel—spent his power slowly collecting
        watches and wrestling
with grooms in the stables—like male otters, they bite each other's necks,
        drawing blood, but

thick layers of fat prevent serious injury. We see only the profile of Doña
        Carlota Joaquina,
the King's eldest daughter, more oversexed than even her mother, whose "chief
        renown was for a readiness

that kept her in a state of tropical humidity as would grow orchids
        in her drawers
in January" ("My mouth may be scalded but I'm still noticeably wet,"
        she wrote a lover.)

                                    •

Tennessee Williams had a little black dog named Bibbles whom
        he kept as a minotaur
keeps his women—he set to kicking it one day because the creature
        seemed to him

too promiscuous, too "Whitmanesque" in its affections. Seventy-one
        and choking
on the cap of a medicine bottle—nothing like the brass bit in a horse's spit-foamed
        mouth, nothing

like the rough-trade neck-ties that had gagged him. Tell us a joke; tell us a story
        to make us all
laugh. The cops: "If that's aspirin on your dresser, what's the needle for?"
        Him: "I can't stand the taste

of the stuff." Tennessee—the eternal that is ever-present in our midst. Sexually
        incontinent. Panic
insomnia, tooth-rot, green liquid pouring from the bowels. Still
        he has a physical

presence. You could imagine him hitting someone. "I don't think it's sex
      I want. There's no great
hankering for that. It's the quiet, humdrum dread of coming up alone to this little
      room at night, to that

emptiness where God would be if God were available. And going to bed and turning
      my face to the wall."

ANOOSH'S OBITUARY FOR HIMSELF, TO HIS SON

Armaan, during the Revolution your mother
left, and I was asked to strangle a collaborator:
baggy-trousered, with a stoat-face. The house's pink wallpaper
was covered with maids and horses. Over the shower curtain
his wife's pantyhose hung. Chair-tied, sweat ran the rims
of his glasses. A lamp threw cold light, promises
were made. I'm a father. Drunk, I adjourned to the driveway
to shovel snow. There were spider webs of moisture
in the trees and hedges. For coffee, I used ice cream
in place of the missing milk, sick of what I knew . . .
As for your mother, Armaan, I can only say I feel better
about her infidelities when I'm well-dressed. And I am.

WINTER NIGHTS

Walking from the house into a field
of snow, the moon eases from its blue

blouse, half-blinded by the hills. Eider
shadows skate past the pond boat

overturned on shore. There is
the fatty scent of pine, like the smell

of marrow. Things are blooming
that shouldn't yet. She reaches up

to her shadowed face to touch
something real but imagined, like

some invented criminal pleasure,
like making a virtue of a flaw.

HIDING AGAIN IN LONDON

The streets, black with rain, I walk
past the British Museum to University College,
        where the Socialist Workers Party is screening *Land and Freedom*.
I sit in the audience, looking
        for women—confusing jargon: class intercourse,

        sexual warfare—aware of the probability
of defeat. We can't know much
        of each other. I fell in love with Marx
several years before, though, in life, he despised
        the lower classes—as we despise ourselves—making him

        one of us. How could he not be—
writing Engels for ten pounds here, twenty pounds
        there. Boils, jaundice, grippe; three children
dead of poverty; bread and potatoes
        for days; and not an unbroken piece of furniture

        in the house. He writes a friend, "I was so depressed
last night that I would have put my head
        in the oven, if I wasn't too frightened of the children
to go into the kitchen. After the anarchists
        and communists lose to Franco the lights

        come up, stout is served in the student annex,
where I talk with two Argentine friends about anything
        but politics or exile, the *añoranza*: soccer mostly, and the black
girl across the room, Elizabeth, who is looking
        at me, and away, and back again. Outside, she tells me

about her professor-parents, her home in Sussex
where sweet William pins itself to the slats of the front porch,
        where she walks out to horse-stables in the morning
in jodhpurs and a tank-top. Then, scattershot
        of car horns—a hand suddenly unpocketed, the hairs

        on our arms touching—even at night, the riot
of poppies in spring. Beside our confused feet
        a lung-sore bum with his *Guardian* tent and cardboard mat
is sleeping, as I push her breasts up beneath her sweater.
        Months like this passed before I left for Stockholm

        carrying the anonymous thing that we've always
known without having learned,
        that we'll lose, that speaking into silence, our gods,
parent-ghosts, and lovers will not
        hear us. Still, call after him. Awkwardly call this man,

        "Bear," of all things, as his family did, through hob
and tobacco smoke—just up from bed, he's still sitting
        in his study on the Isle of Wight, where he has put
his head down, the blue capillaries under skin
        as thin as rice paper, with the hard-focused eyes

        of a man one week at the bottom of a lake—
and what is the vocabulary for that, how
        can words deliver affection; I say it is raining
over the mountains and mean I am rolling onto my side
        to fall asleep next to you.

SLEEPING WITH UNCLE LESTER

We walked from town to her land
through clotted darkness
and frozen pastures, heads brushing
bottles hung on low branches. The old
kitchen, cut by a line of ragged shirts
and socks, smelled like wet bark. Jars
of fruit salts and redcurrants, tins
of dried onions and parsnips rattled
when we walked. We went to bed,
that's all. I woke with her uncle Lester
beside me, slack-chinned and thin, face
and neck a wash of white stubble
and the high turpentine of fetid sweat.
Lester's wife died when their Chrysler
broke down as she hemorrhaged
from miscarriage. I got up
on my elbows; out the window
was the background of an otherwise dull
family photo: blue skies and egg shells
blown across a bald yard, rain pattering
the stinking fine dust, and steam billowing
up from somewhere—a tree
of backlit breath, and Lester's grindy voice
like the cold of close metal, "Hey, dunghill.
Lookit—you're blockin' the view."

THE LEAVING

There is the rain on the copper
roofs, there is the *click-shuff*

of red heels on concrete, the voice
of a ruddy-faced neighbor

above, calling after her husband.
In their apartment, the pillows

still sleep-dented and sour
with breath. The headless straws

of aster stalks hang above
the credenza, beside the battered

front door. There are the bridge's
rust-water icicles, its bands

of moss seaming a forgotten
cobblestone sidewalk. There is

the river in thistle-gray cowlicks,
and the husband above it, deciding.

WINTER INVENTORY

I look out at the river in cakes of ice
sliding violently over one another,

speaking a language remembered
from another of earth's ages, and almost

understand that speech as human, some
body of absence struggling with itself

under bridge lights. And remember
a winter spent driving a heatless car

with a patchwork quilt thrown over my legs
until more than a ghost of warmth existed

and I was alone on a country road under
a nothing sky with stubbled fields

and telephone poles flashing past
and the sense that if I closed my eyes

I might remain sitting, speeding along,
no car, and soon no road, and perhaps

the trees evaporate and the telephone polls
sink deep into hard earth and nothing

then but myself, and a river far off, and the name
of someone, and still no better understanding.

WATER FROM THE SAME SOURCE

Knuckles stripped
           to a skinned goat's head—
      the nearly vacant fingers

of barge workers; when you left
           I was wire-jawed
      and shut-in from surgery.

Going back out, sinking
           into subway tunnels, I was reminded
      how easy it is to forget the world

is inhabited mostly by others.
           I've got three joints
      in my shirt pocket, and we're kicking ash

from our shoes in the pointless
           heat, smashing a ditch's discarded bottles
      in the night, so that their wreck

spreads in cinders over the blacktop
           like silage spilled into moonlight, like
      something you might want.

ELEBADE

When I woke
I felt fine for a minute.

Set the table, saw myself
rise and go. First rise

and stand, holding
the table. Then sit

again. Then go. Start
to go.

Motionless pines
we'd built, stirred.

Blind October
inching up. No wife

raising hell
when she came. Empty

or almost empty beast.
Bull down. Bad heart.

BLIND ATTIS

Her lover was a black bear
whose empty eye-sockets rattled

with pebbles. And though
he should not have existed, she believed

as she believed in stones that fell
from high places. She knew

when he had been with others
because he loped through the pines

and lindens smelling like a mudbound
whale. One night under

the stars strung out behind a haze
of brushfire, he slept clutching

a claw-scratched rosary.
And she climbed, brushing

her stark nakedness along his coarse
length, to the soil-rimmed holes

in his head and found no manic
bestial glow, but the dark

behind cracked lantern slides. And he rose
and like a husband he cut her—

"I will love you more when I am older . . .
if I let you live," she breathed

into his pricked ears. Each night
she took a bit more blood

from him, until he woke
under a crooked moon

and reached to maul her crouching
black figure. But she had taken

his paws, and biting, she whispered
into the folds and long darkness

of his ear, "If you return again it will be
through the eyeholes of birds," for whom

she left the pink jigsaw of his hatcheted
remains steaming in the morning.

SMOKE

I dreamt your childhood wound, softened
in bathwater, had reappeared,
an ochre-blue puncture at the heel—
dimpled star spreading to uneven
points. It held in its shadow
a leaf stem, beetle-brown. I pulled it
from your foot and it brought more leaves
littering the bath. Soon you were
a tub of dogwoods and blackthorns
I gathered and carried out
to the grass between the crocuses
where I stood over you, bit of earth fleeing
into smoke, spelling nothing above the yard.

TIME AWAY

A female cardinal has taken up a limned branch
but her prey has flown inside, with me. Tonight, on the phone

I fought again with my son's mother. She has become
so used to my cruelty that it is simply questioned

and assessed. I used to surprise myself. A friend reads
a story I've written, finding the main character "deplorable."

There are a lot of things I don't tell him. Earlier,
I passed the ostensibly intelligent woman with pock-marked

cheeks, who works at the bookstore down the block, who
has lived here her whole life, so whose only remaining

chances are those who move here, or return after
years away. Out back, sheaves of silverweed and Indian pipe

sink and buckle into mud. During grad school there was a string
of suicides in the school library. One jumper from the atrium

fell silently to land at the feet of my student. She told me
about his breathing, was nervous about taking some time away

from classes, and came to ask if that might be okay. "Yeah,"
I said, "that would be okay." I've moved and come back so many

times. By December the backyard will be a moist cushion
of decay, bits of spider, robin, and mouse carcasses. One day,

I'll pack up what little I own that's unbroken and move
to Montana. For now, I put off going home—there is

nothing but empty conversation, and the historical moment.
The first time my father got in my face, and for once

I came closer, I turned away only to throw
an antique dresser across the bedroom, before inviting him

to hit me—all he could do was threaten to call the cops, the brittle
embarrassing admonishment of middle-age. I feel sure I won't

find anyone, now. I've settled into that a bit. And I find myself
attracted more and more to pregnant women—I'm familiar

with their bodies—the solid, outsized stomachs, and darkened
nipples, and maybe I think this time I could get it right.

THE CHILDREN, THE GRASS

Here are the children, tall as knee-high grass,
    who will climb the mornings into bed with you

to make the day loose and foolish, and the sea
    not so far away. They are soft as warts of moss.

And still they are ignorable, which suits.
    It is not easy to know how best

to move yourself from one place
    to another but they will help.

They rinse your arms, feet and face
    with seawater, provide a pocketful of almonds.

UNDERCOVER

The train to Trieste—Schiele, fifteen,
        hoisting his sister's
    suitcase onto the rack, a wash

of cold light flushing her face like breath
        traveling across
    glass. Lost in fog, the windows

would not give their faces back. Her sleeping feet
        brush the skin above
    his socks, and outside, the honeysuckle

like a pattern of blood repeating itself
        around a fence.
    Lincoln, depressed, flickering

about the edges of the woods for weeks—
        his eyes' snow-lashed
    halo, and his gun—like his uncle Mordecai,

a hermit who kept a dog named Grampus
        and hundreds
    of pigeons—here are their elaborate houses

with gables and columns, far from the double-bed
        above a general store ·
    where Joshua Speed and long Ishmael lie

for four years like brothers. Far from what will swell
                    and blacken
          at Gettysburg. In the glow of low fire on charred brick

sweat-pale Adolf Schiele is laid out,
                    in a railway
          official's dress uniform, syphilitic, a dagger

at his side. Not burning the family's stocks
                    and bonds. Not storming.
          Not breaking down the door to a lightless room

that hides Egon and his sister, his first and best
                    model, simply
          developing film. Plaster cast brains, hydrocephalic

skulls, and weight scales—Alphonse Bertillon comes
                    every workday
          to the *Laboratoire Anthropologie*, to his

father's skeleton hanging from the wall
                    like some mobile
          of the Pleiades, as if the bones' equilibrium

could keep him from slipping beyond reach. Young
                    urchins, three sisters,
          sit in Schiele's studio. They sleep, comb hair,

pick their ears, pull at dresses—the raw mottled
                    flesh of inconvenient
          limbs, bruising, impassive, the vent of ribs beneath

thin skin. John Brown had the eyes of a goat,
                    and beating
          his sons, forced them to strike back

as often as he struck. Brown called his killing
                    "work," watching
          in the late moonlight while his sons

and others knocked as lost travelers on the nightdoors
                    of anti-abolition families
          and cut their men to pieces—like opening

a seed-bag—while the women slept, the ground alive
                    where bodies fell, black
          scars on dark grass, and when it rained the smell

came into the houses. A child
                    with the shambling
          gait of a circus bear, Clyfford Still's family

in South Dakota was digging a well and they needed
                    someone to go down
          to see the condition of the pit. It smelled like

the faint decay of overripe almonds—
        the way his father
    smelled in from the rain, the deep creases of his hands

and coveralls traced with night-crawler soil. "They put
       a rope around my ankle,
    tied a simple knot, and dropped me down head first."

APPREHENDED AT A DISTANCE

The colorless lake—buoy bells
      in fog; groaning, algaed pylons.

The impractical sand, clouds hanging
      in dystrophy. Blue trees below the struts

of a radio telescope. A hare racing
      through the tide. Eels dead and alive

sold from back of a truck. A preacher
      stumbling over a mastiff, like a little man;

the insinuation of a human on a chain—
      the slobbering aperture. A street sweeper

swinging his broom like a scythe. A starling
      speaks and goes. Like someone who has a choice.

SNOW IN A BRICK COURTYARD

On a kitchen window's slate ledge,
a swallow, white chest dusted orange
from the moth in its beak. Across
the courtyard, a black dog perched
atop its house, one ear pricked
to the wind. A rusty nail
sticks up from a sodden
half-buried plank, shocking the snow
with a faint russet pulse. And a child's
distant croup-cough seems to stir
snow from frost-glazed branches.
Here is the cloud-helmeted sun, and here
is the world smoothed and close
to the eyes, like the gleam of cupped hands
bathing a face above a sink's darkening basin.

WINTER FEVER

. . . which even now Jack
was preparing. When he knelt
at the roof's edge and threw
crushed ice over the yard
it began to snow
all over town, and I saw
milk running in sheets
down a blackboard, children swerving
through the darkness
in their underwear,
and Marcus riding the carousel's
bearded seal—bending to whisper
into its ear, his long upper lip
flat and sweating.
It was the coldest night
of the year—the cats were in heat.

THE COW

Snagged in a barbed fence, bands of phlegm
at my lips, having already left

flesh on the humming wire, I imagined
myself capable of standing. With hands

like the absent farmer's—with his vulgar
pride in mediocrity, his waterlogged

pornography, and Great Dane called Hamlet—
instead of these clumsy, mud-clotted hooves.

In work boots—a tattoo of snow in the pattern
of a paddlewheel on my coat—clipping

the farmer and his people above the ankles,
like mallards, from the frozen pond, impaling

them with straightened bedsprings
for posing—their eyes train windows,

blank and daubed with pollen, their bodies thrown
over my shoulder, legs bundled like iris stems.

THE INSOMNIAC

The pig with the black feet is an insomniac.
Long ago kids left a mask filled with leaves
in the yard. Now the insomniac wears it—
leaning his head down, snuffing, it sticks
to his moist snout, and he's Marlon Brando.
We find hidden, delicately stripped orange
skins, candy wrappers, and shredded letters
that name him, Albert. He's like a Russian—
enormous, vulnerable, perhaps tragic—
a lover of darkness: snow-capped trashcans,
coal bins, ships' holds, sinkholes. He wanders
in the nightwoods for days, sending back
sounds like the ripple of radio voices
until it's not Christmas, just one more day
and he hangs by his slick black feet, unzipped,
the warm wet release lipping his chin.
Never indiscriminate in his passions
he understood being human, the chasm
between the classes, but never condescended,
even when he must have known he'd be eaten
on paper plates with potatoes and a couple of carrots.

WE LIVED ABOVE THE KEY SHOP

When I was a child
father came home

with hands for us. Before,
it was our faces

to the plate—now
we could eat

with ease. Our feet
he smuggled home

just in time for us
to begin school. Imagine

my sister and I,
only a spectral space

between our ankles
and cold linoleum. Eyes

came days later
but those he stole

from the Vietnamese
couple down the street—

they screamed after him
in their language

to bury them
at the seashore with crab claws

and the scales of shad. We saw
that first day of classes,

the walleyed cruelty
of our peers—an overweight

boy strapped in
a Miss Somewhere sash—

and something shrunk
inside of us so small

that sparrows were born
from our faces and blew about

until they crumbled and we
caught them on our tongues

but were always unsatisfied—
it's hunger we were born with.

CLEAN LINES, DIFFUSE LIGHTING

Sometimes the old man cut
mother's hair; there were limits even
to his failure. Other times, when
we were in the mood that someone
should pay for what we found
intolerable—field mice, threatening
rain, a shout in the street—he
might even cut himself. He was
so mild he began to snow. It's all
made quite beautiful now, really,
with clean lines and diffuse lighting.

COMING IN AT NIGHT

He butts her, with bathwater in the divot beneath her nose, this cat
of ours, and washes his face of her, fur curled back

like a moist leaf.
                    Between thumb and two fingers I rub his ears, as coarse
with dirt as a snail's etched shell.

                         And here, because of the closeness
of the night sky, cicadas' wings seem enormous, sweeping things.
Far from here, seagulls hover above stairs that descend into water.

We have never been so far from shore.
                         Yesterday, she and I climbed
our house's forest of rafters to the highest windows to see
how much desert we could see.

                         Thistle, thistle, black swallowtail,
cottonwood that signals, finally, a creek nearby that we walk out to,
and watch

          its bottom-layer of detritus, dusted with mud, waves
upward, loosening memories of cold green hills,

                              lamps swinging
over them in darkness. The smell of warm bricks and the rain

on them. And on the mill's dam a shard of broken bottle
flashing, and the black shadow
of our cat rolling by, waiting

for fish heads thrown
into the canal—the creases between my nails and fingers filled
with blood

from the cleaning. Walking in from the porch, she is lying
in bed—like my own hands looked at long enough, she becomes
strange. On the roof the copper vane is tacking in strong wind.

Quiet breathing,
flushed ears, errant hairs thick as wet grass, the webbing
between her forefinger and thumb thin as bleached leaves.

And perhaps later we walk out over the sand, without waking, pounding
out some secret we bury in desert darkness.

WASHING MY OLD MAN

The pads of his palms are cool and mapped
with wet creases like blades of grass. His figure

arranges itself in my head. His is the sleep
of furniture. There were lots of times

I didn't love him. But it's been said I look
like him, or a famous director. The French

always say things are the same when
they aren't, at all. Someone asked him once,

"Which god do you mean?" "Yours,
if you like," he answered. That he was sometimes

horrible and still lived, that he was
often horrible and somehow we loved him.

HE SPEAKS OF OLD AGE

Eighty, I'm up at eight, bathe
        and trifle about until lunch. After,
I have a cup of bourbon and coffee,

It makes my mind race. I'm seeking
        help. Do I get breathless when I exercise?
I'd hardly know. I have reached the age

now when my daughter can beat me
        at croquet. It took me a long time
to become a human being. I can't say

I have a lot of hope
        for the whole thing. I procrastinate
by answering email. My neighbors

judge me now entirely on the cut
        of my coat; but we're all equally poor
so the verdict is softly given.

Beside my bed the radio plays; I read
        Malone muert. My world is fairly floorboardish.
Outside, the drab reiteration

of brickwork, dahlias spring
        from a moldering mattress, charred
timber litters the leaf-brindled rainwater.

My favorite room is the kitchen,
        though I've given up on eating—
I've gotten to where I don't like

to have food in my mouth, and heaven
        is the moment after constipation.
I've grown not ugly, but entirely

unattractive. Bathing now, my eyes
        are drawn to the wide-wrinkled, two-potato
sack at my crotch. Though, you'll be

happy to know, even now my sex life could
        fill more than one wet holiday weekend. Still,
passive as a toilet, I want my God back.

HIS DEMENTIA

Hands clapped flat between
        knees I slept as the old man
shuffled through the French doors
        and grabbed my shoulder—

rolling over, he slipped his hand
        into mine—skin like black cabbage,
the skin of one badly burnt.
        He leaned close—eyes green marbles

under ice, and I could see beside
        the long darkness of his ear's tunnel,
a blue sore like a decomposing berry,
        and he said that he wanted Houdini

in the Hippodrome with Jennie
        the elephant, and his black stack
of scratchy Red Seal albums
        for the crank Victrola, and the dunes

and cut & pressed glass ruins
        of a coastal town. I let him into bed,
and we listened a long time
        to the furnace—I sang Caruso

into his good ear, until he began nodding
        and I escaped from my skin leaving it
beside an old, deaf, nearly-blind man,
        a palsied pile of nylons, a world of snow.

IN MOURNING

My father was inconsiderate enough
to die. A barrister, he loved
his wig. The criminals liked it too. No one wants
to be sent to prison by someone wearing
a t-shirt. They cut his carotid in autopsy
and asked if we had a scarf he might wear
for the funeral. So he lies in state
like Liberace. The rings won't fit
the swollen fingers. On his sixtieth
he planted his face in the cake. When
the undertaker isn't around I run him through
the range of motions—the pulleys
and cranes of his knees still creak. I've never
seen god in the face of a sleeping girl
or anywhere else. The old lovely bastard.

NOW AND FOREVER

I'm not wary of myself, or others,
but myself in the presence
of others. It might be safest
to stay home and read. Saturn's rings
become the cast-iron balcony
of a house seen from everywhere,
on which inhabitants of the planet
take the air in the evening.
None of us is more alone
than another, and still no comfort
in it. I have never clutched anything . . .
at dusk deliriously. Sunlight
on stones is nothing like laughter
and still there is nearly enough.

FÅRÖ

After Ingmar Bergman's *The Passion of Anna*

The snag of meeting new people
is that you're asked to care about them—

nightmares, affairs, surgeries. Outside,
twenty-five sheepbells like wind chimes.

Nail bucket won't stay on the roof. Boys hung
a small dog from a low branch—it's cries covered

by gulls. Got the noose knot right. Took him
down live. That night I'm invited to dinner; tie

and black jacket. Swedish gin, discreet charm. Two
women with overbites god-talking, and a job

in a turtleneck. Shadowed interiors before snow-lit
casements. Leave a door ajar and there are

questions. Miss a fellow's funeral, the bones'll
never know. Frost-eaten pinecones. Muck-boots

in the green wetwhite goose shit, passing a butchers'
rack: lamb flanks, hog's heads, a small shack humid

with horse piss and fish. If a rocks glass is thick
enough it makes a good sound when it breaks.

THE KINGHORSE BUTCHERTOWN BRAWL

Fifteen and scared, stabbing
a thick-necked skinhead

in Solovairs and a mule coat—
the quick resistance and crack,

sound like a hoof on gravel. He davened
back on his heels. The dumb, bird-shot

shock of his mouth
and the boggy slot, petering out

a bloody puddle. I rolled my tongue
around in my mouth a second,

then split. After twenty blocks
of cold I stopped

to wipe my hands and felt bad
but not sorry yet.

DAKOTA

They took him
in their car

to the 4400 block
of _____ Avenue,

near the airport,
where they left him

behind a utility
shed. The older

one driving. They
put a plastic bag

over his head
before they shot him

above the left ear. He
must have thought

they were going
to suffocate him.

A POLITE HISTORY

Walking through ice-seamed streets
to a theater, a streetcar full of talking
bodies passed a woman, before a column
of tanks rolling towards the town square
to confront a revolt. The woman
waved at the soldiers, and at that moment
she was tempted for the first time to join
them. It was not that the woman, with her
small breakable nose, tolerated the cruelty
of such a struggle in the hope
that it would bring a prosperous future:
the harshness of the violence was simply
endorsed as a sign of authenticity, three
or four times bigger than an opera.

THE REVOLUTION

The signal was a girl's raised
gloved hand to her red hair. So, it spread
along the rye fields, through the alfalfa
and dusty roads, to our homes, like birds
barking in the hollows of the hills. We were
rebels; or when generals were killed,
the generals. Sometimes the military
were better rebels. We were the products
of our own ideas: being rough
is a game. Unseen loudspeakers drowned
protest in canned laughter and waltzes. Men
patched wounded women; like pregnancy
it was an unfair competition. Captured
or capturing, condemnation followed
upon execution. What's lovely about war
is its devotion to thoroughness
and order. It keeps count. At the end
we got down and tasted the forest floor,
holding the place where someone
was before, stood in dead shoes,
understanding the mathematics of it, the finite
sets of odd cardinality, below the pirated
nest of a titmouse and eight pink-white eggs.

DIORAMA—(SCARLET AND LIVER)

There is Mussolini in his tight,
                              rough-wood coffin,
shirtless on pine shavings. One eye opened. Swollen face
pancaked, his mouth a singed, lipless stretch.

                              •

"Despisal of the bourgeois is the beginning of virtue. . . ," wrote Flaubert.

and wondered why we laugh
at affliction.
              Maybe it's because that thing
that sits with us at breakfast—
                              that eland—and looks back at us
from the bathroom mirror, and sleeps
                              even in our coat pockets,
that thing intimate and unfamiliar, a someone
unknown
              who we will enter or be entered by, *is*,
finally.

                              •

The miniature American flag waves
from the blue, snow-stranded Bronco's antenna.

                              •

The fascists were hung by their feet—like the crooks and embezzlers
of medieval times—

                from the girders of an *Esso* gas station
in the *Piazzale Loreto*. A far cry from the Mussolini
who sat in a chair at cocktail parties

                        holding his thumb out
for women to bite down hard on.

                    Closer to Goya's *Suerte de Varas*
whose arena is littered with gored horses,
and a picador frozen amid a frenzied crowd

                      who stare at the bull,
its wounded shoulder a bloodburst,
balancing against stupor.

          Out of decency
before the crowd in the *Piazzale* abused the bodies,
Clara Petacci's skirt was tied tightly around her knees.

           •

My great grandmother's death

                was communicated to me by phone
through an impatient orderly—"Mrs. _____ has expired"—

                        as if
she were a side of beef

         or an embrace between lovers in an English gazebo.

           •

Flaubert also said: "The most beautiful woman isn't

                                             beautiful at all

                 on the dissecting table, with her bowels

on her face,

              one leg flayed, and an extinct cigar

                                  reposing

on her foot."

                          •

Turn the picture upside down

                       and the seven hanging fascists

with their arms outstretched

                    look much like their excited countrymen

screaming for a goal at the Stadio San Siro.

                          •

          Fritz Haber

                whose fertilizers increased the world's food supply

sevenfold—*Brod aus Luft*;

                  whose gasses strangled allied troops in the trenches

of Ypres—*Tod aus Luft*;

                 whose wife, soon after, shot herself

in the heart with his service revolver, and the bullet

                        passing through her

made a sound like the gulls

              baying outside.

•

There are men on the Esso station's girders, communist partisans,

                                        looking down

the bodies of the hanging dead,

                    as relaxed as steelworkers arguing baseball,

lighting cigarettes on a single steel beam, seventy stories

                               above Manhattan

in Ebbets' *Lunch on a Skyscraper*. It's the curling

fingers that give the dead away

                    as if in reaching for snow

instead they found sandpaper.

SARCLET

A gull with one wing dragging like a banner
humps down the ice-skinned cove. A thinning
man among the raw-boned cows, nostrils wide, salt burn.
Lung-colored water breaks like one hundred doors
slamming, shrinking shingles, and away.
Fat snow butts a fallen gutter. The overlong
cold-droozed grass slips from chapped hands thickening
in the naked wind, falling asleep at the line, sliding
darkly into pockets. As the eyes loosen
their bluish hold on the horizon, killdeer cut
over the dunes—the sky's market light, the sun kneeling
between clouds in thin complicated continents.

THE MAYOR IN SKY-BLUE SOCKS

Deer herd in the icy fields. The mayor
        in sky-blue socks hugs a chestnut,

biting the bark like a cube of sugar
        between his teeth, but no tea coming,

just polite hatred, holding the place
        where someone else had been, too dumb

even to scream. No one will ever love him
        as that cat loved him. In this place night vanishes

men from the world; it's no safer, nor
        more attractive, but it's improved appreciably.

THE BIRTHDAY PARTY

Morning ferry
after a night

of carnations,
a deserved toast.

Now, the rail station
burning. Too much

wind and cigarettes.
Green night

in my hair. Eyes
all over.

A STRAPPING BOY

After Jean Genet's The Thief's Journal

I was the theatre
of a fairyland

restored to life.
When the waltz ended,
the two soldiers

disengaged themselves.
And each of those two

halves of a solemn
and dizzy block
hesitated, and happy

to be escaping
from invisibility,

went off, downcast,
toward some girl
for the next waltz.

ORR'S ISLAND

So small
my neighbor

last autumn. Shadow
lake. Moon half.

Light
save us. Shade

his backlit
outline. His dead

ages. Who'd fail
his girl of sixteen—

his son, Vietnam,
god, reason? He'd

sit out there
in the wind, come

dark. Long dead.

UNEASE

The sun wore out
the mesh of morning
air, wind pitched
among weeds, the hum
of ducks like government
buildings. The swelling
perfectly upholstered
nursing home, the trees
sucking at the heat.
Monkfish on ice above
the slow, slick fluid
at the curb. Cabs go on
moving over the streets
like a fog, as if invisible,
as the beaked policeman
idiotically crosses himself.

COMPORTMENT

From such material it is almost
        impossible to create a picture

of life. What was the color
        of the travel permit a sergeant

would have needed to get from spring
        to fall that year? One strips for oneself,

a kind of masochistic self-inspection
        with a scarlet-billed crane outside

the window. A natural celibate,
        a kind of anchorite. An event

at the limits. Outside, daylight sits
        shining beneath the fog above an island

like water on a rabbit's ear. The body
        is useful, then isn't. One goes

and sits at the mahogany desk
        as if nothing has happened.

CONDENSATION CUBE

After David Alworth's "Bombsite Specificity."

The best way to visit Kelvedon Hatch bomb shelter is in the new
        Alfa-Romeo. With its four-wheel disc brakes,
luxurious interior and road-holding ability, it's safe, fast and pleasant
        to drive. Just follow the sign: "Secret

Nuclear Bunker." '60's-era mannequins in Burberry with moving legs
        and breasts, loitering in corridors. A skinny husband
in the craw of a cold bed, with a snore like a toothache. Tranquil tensions
        escalated. With striptease the décor is always

more important than the person disrobing. Whatever chaos reigns above—fallow
        fields, the ponds cowering—
life underground is snappy, ordered, austere. A zone of leisure. How war can be
        productive; constellating Nixon in the kitchen, celebrating appliances

and amenities. Baked beans, tomato juice, Nescafé, a rational level
        of dread. Outside, night's cold,
object's cold; no different from a church. Condensation on Plexiglas. Descending
        from a slope of debris, children swarm

the ruins. False-feathered cardinals for floral arrangements, pressed
        & colored glassware, garden
tools. Typhoid from seashells cleaned improperly. How stupid and forgettable
        adults are. To conceive of the world

as a target. Like a cantilevered goldfish. To vie for spots in the only shelter
        in the neighborhood. Nowhere else
to go but another part of the airplane. To photograph ourselves as humans; to see
        ourselves as bullets and bombs

see us. Children embroidered in a rug like musical instruments abandoned
in a field. Seeing all the different moments
the way we can look at a stretch of the Rocky Mountains; like soldiers looting a clock
factory. Participant-observers; innocent

nobodies. The incompleteness of the past; the ongoingness of history. Dogs eating grass
beneath the dripping trees; the smell
of a white dress rained on. It is a country which you can imagine, for it is
pretty like a picture, as it lies there

amidst its landscape, like an artisanal snow-globe, which it owns.

NOTES

"Combine" owes a debt to the following:
>Inside the Stalin Archives: Discovering the New Russia by Jonathan Brent
>Wyatt Prunty's forward to The Selected Poems of Howard Nemerov
>Tom Stoppard's Arcadia
>John Worthen's D.H. Lawrence: The Life of an Outsider
>Peter Hall in "Demolition Man: Harold Pinter and The Homecoming," by John
>>Lahr, in The New Yorker
>"Anne Carson, The Art of Poetry #88," in The Paris Review, interview by Will
>>Aitken

"Anoosh's Obituary for Himself, to His Son" features a small detail taken from an apocryphal story of Robert Creeley being served coffee with ice cream in place of cream by Louis Zukofsky.

"Winter Nights" contains a phrase reconfigured from Knut Hamsun's Pan.

"Hiding Again, in London" owes a debt to:
>Edmund Wilson's To the Finland Station
>"Becoming the Emperor: How Marguerite Yourcenar Reinvented the Past," by
>>Joan Acocella, in The New Yorker
>The Mrs. Woolf and the Servants: The Hidden Heart of Domestic Service, by
>>Alison Light

"Sleeping with Uncle Lester" borrows particulars from David Cone's Scott of the Antarctic: A Life of Courage and Tragedy in the Extreme South.

"Elebade" borrows from Samuel Beckett's last prose piece, Stirrings Still.

"Undercover" features details from:
>Joshua Wolf Shenk's Lincoln's Melancholy: How Depression Challenged a
>>President and Fueled His Greatness

Frank Whitford's *Egon Schiele*

Jennifer Michael Hecht's *The End of the Soul: Scientific Modernity, Atheism, and Anthropology in France*

David S. Reynolds' *John Brown, Abolitionist*

"Unfurling the Hidden Work of a Lifetime," by Seven Henry Madoff, in *The New York Times*

"Apprehended at a Distance" owes a debt to Elfriede Jelinek's Nobel Lecture, and Virginia Woolf's *Orlando*.

"Clean Lines, Diffuse Lighting" borrows from E.L. Doctorow's *The Book of Daniel*.

"He Speaks of Old Age" quotes briefly from:

"Domains: Sir John Mortimer: The Country Barrister," by Edward Lewine, in *The New York Times*

Elfriede Jelinek's *Lust*

William Feaver's *Lucien Freud*

John Berryman quoting from a conversation he had with W.B. Yeats, as appears in "John Berryman, The Art of Poetry #16," in *The Paris Review*, interview by Peter A. Stitt

"In Mourning" features detail from "Domains: Sir John Mortimer: The Country Barrister," by Edward Lewine, in *The New York Times*.

"Now and Forever" features particulars from Walter Benjamin's *Arcades Project*, and Maurice Merlea-Ponty's *Phenomenology of Perception*.

Fårö is a small Baltic Sea island north of the island of Gotland, off Sweden's southeastern coast, on which Ingmar Bergman both lived and filmed many of his movies.

"A Polite History" uses specifics from Slavoj Zizek's *Welcome to the Desert of the Real*, and from the Graywolf anthology, *New European Poets*, edited by Wayne Miller and Kevin Prufer.

"The Revolution" borrows from Gaston Bachelard's *The Poetics of Space*, and "Putin's Pariah," by Andrew Meier in *The New York Times*. It also briefly paraphrases Walter Benjamin's essay "Central Park," one of his many writings on Baudelaire.

"Diorama—(Scarlet and Liver)" features detail from Tom Stoppard's *Arcadia*.

Sarclet is a small crofting village near Wick on the eastern coast of the Scottish Highlands.

"Comportment" utilizes specifics from:
    Beatrice Hanssen's writing on Elfriede Jelinek's *The Piano Teacher* in *Critique of Violence*
    Anthony Cronin's *No Laughing Matter: The Life and Times of Flann O'Brien*
    Saul Friendlander's *Probing the Limits of Representation: Nazism and the "Final Solution"*

"Condensation Cube" takes its name, and perhaps more, from the art object of the same name by Hans Haacke. It further borrows from:
    Jean-luc Godard's *Pierre le Fou*
    Joseph Heller's *Catch-22*
    Tom Clark's poem "Like musical instruments"
    Kurt Vonnegut's *Slaughterhouse-Five*
    David Alworth's "Site Specificity"

Michael Winters

Adam Day is the recipient of a Poetry Society of America Chapbook Fellowship for *Badger, Apocrypha*, a PEN Emerging Writers Award, and an Al Smith Fellowship from the Kentucky Arts Council. His work has appeared in *Boston Review, The Kenyon Review, American Poetry Review, Poetry London, AGNI, The Iowa Review, Poetry Ireland, Guernica,* and elsewhere. He coordinates The Baltic Writing Residency in Latvia, Scotland, and the Bernheim Arboretum & Research Forest.

Sarabande Books thanks you for the purchase of this book; we do hope you enjoy it! Founded in 1994 as an independent, nonprofit, literary press, Sarabande publishes poetry, short fiction, and literary nonfiction—genres increasingly neglected by commercial publishers. We are committed to producing beautiful, lasting editions that honor exceptional writing, and to keeping those books in print. If you're interested in further reading, take a moment to browse our website at sarabandebooks.org. There you'll find information about other titles; opportunities to contribute to the Sarabande mission; and an abundance of supporting materials including audio, video, a lively blog, and our Sarabande in Education program.